THI

THE TRUTH,

and

THE LIFE

Jesus is the Only
Way to Heaven

WILLIAM E. VARGAS

Trilogy Christian Publishers
A Wholly Owned Subsidary of Trinity Broadcasting Network
2442 Michelle Drive
Tustin, CA 92780

10 9 8 7 6 5 4 3 2 1
Library of Congress Cataloging-in-Publication Data is available.
ISBN 979-8-89333-358-9
ISBN (ebook) 979-8-89333-359-6

TABLE OF CONTENTS

DEDICATION

I thank God Almighty for the work He has done in my heart, for inspiring me to write this book for His glory.

PREFACE

In 1978, when I was only twelve years old, I accepted the Lord Jesus Christ as Lord and Savior. I was very involved in church activities, and I really enjoyed everything about church. Subconsciously, I always felt like I didn't belong in my country or even in the world. It was a feeling that I have up to this day. Ever since I accepted Jesus as Savior, I always knew I had a few talents (writing, drawing, management of personnel, and mechanical ability) that God Almighty had given me, the most important being writing (which I dislike). I was a good mechanic, troubleshooting and building automation equipment, I managed a maintenance department, but writing, I didn't know how to use it and for what. Writing, however, has given me lots of pats on the back, in college and at work. All these conflicts with different talents have brought me to today.

It is hard to deny that we are living in the last days referred by the scriptures, which is actually the prelude to the second coming of Jesus. In a world that has abandoned God and has embraced the enemy, it has become even more challenging for the church to attract new followers. We are most definitely living in a fallen world, a world that is consumed making boys into women and women into men. It ushes and implements agendas from people who have not been elected by anyone to dictate to society what to do, without even asking for their opinion. In addition, there are a few multibillionaire individuals that choose to use their wealth for the advancement of the anti-Christ agenda. None of this is a surprise. The apostle Paul mentioned our situation in his epistles. In Romans chapter 1 he says the following:

> "Therefore God also gave them up to uncleanliness, in the lusts of their hearts, to dishonor their bodies among themselves, who exchanged the truth of God for the lie, and worshiped and serve the creature rather than the creator, who is blessed forever. Amen. For this reason God gave them up to vile passions. For even their women exchanged the natural use for what is against nature. Likewise also the men, leaving the natural use of the woman, burned in their lust for one another, men with men committing what is shameful, and receiving in themselves the penalty of their error which was due. And even as they did not like to retain God in their knowledge, God gave them over to a debased (or reprobate) mind, to do those things which are not fitting; being filled with all unrighteousness, sexual immorality, wickedness, covetousness, maliciousness; full of envy, murder, strife, evil-mindedness; they are whisperers, backbiters, haters of God, violent, proud, boasters, inventors of evil things, disobedient to parents, undiscerning,

unmerciful; who, knowing the righteous judgement of God, that those who practice such things are deserving of death, not only do the same but also approve of those who practice them." (Romans 1:24-32)

If these things don't describe our society today, I don't know what does.

Going back to my opening paragraph, regarding writing, I always had a sensation, a gut feeling, that God wanted me to use that talent for something, but I couldn't clearly see in what way. I was so distracted with the things of the world that I was being unkowingly rebellious by not giving God the time to show me the way He wanted me to use the talent He had given me. I cared more about the world, using God's blessings that He had given me for my own pleasures and delights, until He had to intervene before I was lost. On October 7th, 2023, I was diagnosed with stage four metastatic colorectal cancer with signet ring, the worst and most deadly form of cancer. Only 2% of the cancer population gets this type. It was then that my eyes opened and I realized that God wanted me to work for His kingdom and bring as many souls as I could to Jesus, so they could be saved. With prayers to God to let the Holy Spirit guide me through this journey, I've been able to move forward in completing this book, and perhaps many more. We are living in such a backwards world that it is mindboggling to understand this philosophy of culture. It seems like it is their way or no way in everything they believe in. According to them, we are supposed to stay in our lane and not color outside the lines. We as the church of Christ need to fight back with the Word of God, to try to bring people to their senses.

ACKNOWLEDGEMENT

I am very grateful for the encouragement and support of my fiancé, Lois, who very gracefully and diligently motivated me to finish the book ahead of time. She helped with ideas and proofreading the book.

Our profound gratitude goes to TBN, to Rachel Hiatt and everyone else involved in this project, for giving me the opportunity to get this book published. I hope it brings many people to Christ.

We are very appreciative of the help and support that Stacy Baker has given us, and for her kindness and professionalism.

May God bless us all.

CHAPTER ONE
THE WAY, THE TRUTH, AND THE LIFE

God bless you, brothers and sisters, for letting me share the scriptures with you through this book, for the glory of the Most-High God, Jehovah (that is God's name), and Jesus Christ, the Lamb of God that takes away the sins of the world, and for the glory of the Holy Spirit who guides us, and Who has directed me to write, always adhering to the scriptures.

The main purpose of my message to you through my writing is for you to understand that Jesus is the only way to be saved and go to heaven. There's no other way. Also, for you not to be deceived by other doctrines promising salvation any other way. Salvation cannot be obtained any other way than through Jesus Christ. Get your Bibles ready.

Jesus said that He was the way the truth and the life, and that no one comes to the Father except through Him. The way I understand this statement, the only way to go to heaven, which is where God resides, is through Jesus Christ.

> *"I am the way, the truth, and the life. No one comes to the father except through me."*
> **John 14:6**

In addition to this verse, who really doesn't remember one of the most popular verses in history, what Jesus said to His apostles in the Gospel of John. This verse is well known around the world by many people:

> *"For God so loved the world that He gave His only begotten Son, that whoever believes in Him should not perish but have everlasting life."*
> **John 3:16**

In addition to John 3:16, Jesus mentioned another important truth in the next verse He tells us that God the Father sent Him to the world, so the world could be saved through Him, and not to condemn the world.

> *"For God did not send His Son into the world to condemn the world, but that the world through Him might be saved."*
> **John 3:17**

So, what does save mean? Well, it simply means what it says. To get to where the Father is, we can only do it by believing in what Jesus said. Some of you might think, why? What about good deeds, good works, and being good, helping others, obeying the Ten Commandments and all that. Does all that count? Well, yes, but good deeds alone will not get us into heaven. James mentioned this in his epistle:

> *"For as the body without the spirit is dead, so faith without works is dead also."*
>
> **James 2:26**

This verse tells us that the only way to be saved and go to heaven is by faith in Jesus Christ, with good works in addition, so good works do count. Jesus puts it in simple terms what to do if we really want to follow Him:

> *"Then Jesus said to His disciples, 'If anyone desires to come after Me, let him deny himself, and take up his cross, and follow Me. For whoever desires to save his life will lose it, but whoever loses his life for My sake will find it.'"*
>
> **Matthew 16:24-25**

We have to take this one step at a time. The last thing I want is to mislead anyone or steer someone in the wrong direction, like the notorious prosperity preachers do. In order to understand salvation and the way to heaven, we need to start by reviewing the book of Genesis, which we will review in chapter 2, where it all started, just to have a good solid understanding of Jesus' bold statements. It can get confusing if you're not familiar with the scriptures. I'll do my best to explain these things. I suggest having a Bible handy to verify whether or not what I'm presenting to you is accurate.

There are a few other things Jesus said to the disciples besides the requirements for salvation we've already reviewed. One was confession of sins mentioned by John and James. Moreover, Jesus also mentioned baptism to His disciples in the Gospels of Mathew and John. In addition, the apostle Paul mentioned to the Ephesians about salvation by grace. Some of the following events took place after Jesus' resurrection; just as a note for those who are not familiar with the scriptures.

> *"If we confess our sins, He is faithful and just to forgive us our sins and to cleanse us from all unrighteousness."*
>
> **1 John,1:9**

> *"Confess your trespasses to one another and pray for one another, that you may be healed. The effective, fervent prayer of a righteous man avails much."*
>
> **James 5:16**

> *"Go therefore and make disciples of all the nations, baptizing them in the name of the Father and the Son and the Holy Spirit."*
>
> **Matthew 28:19**

"Nicodemus said to Him, 'How can a man be born again when he is old? Can he enter a second time into his mother's womb and be born?' Jesus answered, 'Most assuredly, I say to you, unless one is born of water and the Spirit, he cannot enter the Kingdom of God. That which is born of the flesh is flesh, and that who is born of the spirit is spirit. Do not marvel that I said to you, 'you must be born again.'"

John 3:4-7

"And you He made alive, who were dead in trespasses and sins, in which you once walked according to the course of this world, according to the prince of the power of the air, the spirit who now works in the sons disobedience, among whom also we all once conducted ourselves in the lusts of our flesh, fulfilling the desires of the flesh and of the mind, and were by nature children of wrath, just as the others. But God, who is rich in mercy, because of His great love with which He loved us, even when we were dead in trespasses, made us alive together with Christ (by grace you have been saved) and raised us up together and made us sit together in the heavenly places in Christ Jesus, that in the ages to come He might show the exceeding riches of His grace in His kindness toward us in Christ Jesus. For by grace you have

been saved through faith, and that not of yourselves; it is the gift of God, not of works, lest anyone should boast. For we are His workmanship, created in Christ Jesus for **good works**, *which God prepared beforehand that we should walk in them."*

Ephesians 2:1-10

Many of you are wondering in which order we should do these things. Well, in my humble understanding and opinion, 1) we should accept Jesus Christ as our Lord and Savior. 2) We must confess our sins, preferably to God. Perhaps you might want to speak to the pastor of a church, for guidance and understanding. 3) Devote our time and energy to the scriptures and learn the truth. 4) Attend church frequently and get baptized in the name of the Father and the Son and the Holy Spirit.

Once Christ is in you, your actions should speak louder than words; act like Jesus and proclaim the Gospel boldly and without fear, with the help of the Holy Spirit who will dwell within you. God knows this world needs representatives and ambassadors of His Kingdom. It is not an easy task, especially in this world we're living in, full of backwards views and ideas and rebellious attitudes toward the Creator and His church. Let's not allow the enemy to intimidate us and put the spirit of fear in us. The ruler of this world has been defeated. Paul says in his second letter to Timothy not to be afraid, for God has not given us the spirit of fear:

For God has not given us a spirit of fear, but of power and of love and of a sound mind."
2 Timothy 1:7

We as Christians need to be courageous and proclaim the good news, the Gospel of Jesus Christ, without fear and with faith in our Savior. In Acts, Jesus tells Paul not to be afraid but to speak and not keep silent.

"Now the Lord spoke to Paul by the night in a vision, 'Do not be afraid, but speak, and do not keep silent; for I am with you, and no one will attack you to hurt you; for I have many people in this city.'"
Acts 18:9-10

Brothers and sisters, we are living in difficult times. The United States of America has lost its way and moral compass; it has let dark forces and doctrines of demons dominate our society, as the apostle Paul predicted and warned us about in Ephesians 6:11-17. We have become the new Sodom, through a well-planned agenda designed by the enemy. America was infiltrated a long time ago. The enemy is an eternal being, so it does not matter to him if he takes his time for the agenda to be fully implemented in the world, taking generations to be fulfilled. It all started by infiltrating the education system, polluting our children's minds with nonsense and Godless doctrines, getting into the minds of our children to create a separation and division in the family nucleus, especially the families that have no spiritual belief or guidance from a church. In addition to all that, it would not be a bad idea (for the enemy) to dictate what our children watch on television, which is another way to indoctrinate our children and adults, including parents. Owning the companies who decide what we watch on television was another tactic to really get society scrambled; this includes news channels also, the so-called media.

So far, we have discerned that control of the education system, television, and media have already taken place. How about the healthcare and financial systems? Well, they have been infiltrated also. Big pharma is big business, and very profitable too; there are cures for all sickness and diseases. God created us with perfect bodies that will fight any attacks. But if a cure is put out there, then the business will fail. The financial system is for the elites, or servants of the enemy, where the average Joe will never get rich, unless you are chosen to disprove that the markets are for the elites, and created to take the money out of the hand of the average investor. We are living in very dangerous times that will need the protection and guidance of the Almighty God, through our Lord Jesus and the Holy Spirit. Unfortunately, our churches have been infiltrated also. I will talk about that in the coming chapters. Most definitely, the love in people has cooled off like Jesus mentioned. Let's read from Ephesians 6 and Mathew 24.

"Put on the whole armor of God, that you may be able to stand against the wiles of the devil. For we do not wrestle against flesh and blood, but against principalities, against powers, against the rulers of the darkness of this age, against spiritual hosts of wickedness in the heavenly places. Therefore take up the whole armor of God, that you may be able to withstand in the evil day, and having done all, to stand. Stand therefore, having girded your waist with truth, having put on the breast-plate of righteousness, and having shod your feet with the preparation of the gospel of peace; above all, taking the shield of faith with which you will be able to quench all the fiery darts of the wicked one. And take the helmet of salvation, and the sword of the Spirit, which is the word of God."

Ephesians 6:11-17

"And because lawlessness will abound, the love of many will grow cold. 13 But he who endures to the end shall be saved."

Matthew 24:12-13

We can see how our society has changed rapidly; it has become filled with violent haters of the truth, any truth, where only their distorted view of the world is their truth and reality, completely ungodly and oblivious to God's existence. The truth is that we really are in the last days, and we need to come to Christ to be saved.

In the next chapter, we'll be talking about how much God loves us, the origin of sin, and why the sacrifice Jesus endured on the cross was necessary.

God bless you.

CHAPTER TWO

THE FALL OF MAN

The fall of man is a very disappointing event in history, which not only made us mortals, but it also gave women birth pains. We are going to start from where all began, which has been written in the book of Genesis. Reading these accounts will give us a good solid understanding of what happened in the garden of Eden and why we inherit the sin from Adam, which made us all sinners from birth. In Genesis, the author tells us that in the fifth day of God's creation, God said the following:

> *"Then God said, 'Let Us make man in Our image, according to Our likeness; let them have dominion over the fish of the sea, over the birds of the air, and over the cattle, over all the earth and over every creeping thing that creeps on the earth.'"*
> **Genesis 1:26V**

In the next chapter, the author (Moses) tells us how man was formed:

"And the Lord God formed man of the dust of the ground and breathed into his nostrils the breath of life; and man became a living being."

Genesis 2:7

The next verses from chapters 2 and 3 in the book of Genesis will tell us in detail what God's expectations were when He placed man in the garden of Eden. Chapters 2 and 3 of Genesis will also give us a complete picture of God's conditions for Adam and his wife Eve. We'll also see why God disapproves of divorce. Once a man and a woman are united in matrimony, they become one flesh:

"Then the Lord God took the man and put him in the garden of Eden to tend and keep it. And the Lord God commended the man, saying, 'Of every tree of the garden you may freely eat; but of the tree of the knowledge of good and evil you shall not eat, for in the day that you eat of it you shall surely die.'"

Genesis 2:15-17

"And the Lord God caused a deep sleep to fall on Adam, and he slept; and He took one of his ribs, and closed up the flesh in its place. Then the rib which the Lord God had taken from man He made into a woman, and He brought her to the man. Then Adam said: 'This is now bone of my bones And flesh of my flesh; She should be called Woman, Because

she was taken out of man.' Therefore a man shall leave his father and mother and be joined to his wife, and they shall become one flesh."

Genesis 2:21-24

God's instructions were very straightforward: work on the garden and keep it in good shape, eat from all the trees in the garden, except for the tree of knowledge of good and evil. So, what could go wrong? Well, we'll find out in the next verses of Genesis chapter 3:

"Now the serpent was more cunning than any beast of the field which the LORD God had made. And he said to the woman, 'Has God indeed said, "you shall not eat of every tree in the garden?"' And the woman said to the serpent, 'We may eat the fruit of the trees in the garden; But of the fruit of the tree which is in the midst of the garden, God has said, "You shall not eat it, nor shall you touch it, lest you die."' Then the serpent said to the woman, 'You will not surely die. For God knows that in the day you eat of it your eyes will be opened, and you will be like God, knowing good and evil.' So when the woman saw that the tree was good for food, that it was pleasant to the eyes, and a tree desirable to make one wise, she took of its fruit and ate. She also gave to her husband with her, and he ate."

Genesis 3:1-6

This, brothers and sisters, was the fall of man. *Disobedience/rebellion, the original sin.* The Devil, in the form of a serpent, convinced the woman to eat from the forbidden tree in the garden of Eden (this is where the new world order started). The devil, to this day, keeps on collecting souls by lying to them, promising the world to them and misleading them. Greedy poor souls who the devil is giving everything their hearts desire, not for free but in exchange for their souls. We see it on TV, artists confessing that they have sold their soul to the devil. Movie stars, singers, athletes, you name it, he's got his hands on every aspect of our lives. How about the fake media who follow a script and are given the word of the day, or the theme of the day, and they follow it like little puppets. "Fake news." You can say that again. Unfortunately, people are very naive when it comes to the seriousness of their choices in the matter. Selling your soul? To begin with, the soul doesn't belong to us, since it was created by God; therefore, it belongs to God. We are most definitely living in the last days. Thank You, God, for that. Our Lord Jesus Christ is about to return very shortly; that is our hope as Christians.

We are going to keep referencing the book of Genesis to see what follows after Adam and Eve did not obey God's commands. We will continue reviewing chapter 3.

" Then the eyes of both of them were opened, and they knew that they were naked; and

they sewed fig leaves together and made themselves coverings."

Genesis 3:7

"Then the LORD God called to Adam and said to him, 'Where are you?' So he said, 'I heard Your voice in the garden, and I was afraid because I was naked; and I hid myself.' And He said, 'Who told you were naked? Have you eaten from the tree I commanded you that you should not eat?' And the man said, 'The woman whom You gave to be with me, she gave me of the tree, and I ate.' And the LORD God said to the woman, 'What is this you have done?' The woman said, 'The serpent deceived me, and I ate.'"

Genesis 3:9-13

"To the woman He said: 'I will greatly multiply your sorrow and your conception; In pain you shall bring forth children; Your desire shall be for your husband, and he shall rule over you.' Then to Adam He said, 'Because you have heeded the voice of your wife, and have eaten from the tree of which I commanded you, saying, "You shall not eat of it:" Cursed is the ground for your sake; In toil you should eat of it all the days of your life. Both thorns and thistles it shall bring forth for you, and you shall eat the herb of the field. In the sweat of your face you shall

eat bread till you return to the ground, for out of it you were taken; for dust you are, and to dust you shall return.'"

Genesis 3:16-19

"Then the LORD God said, 'Behold, the man has become like one of Us, to know good and evil. And now, lest he put out his hand and take also of the tree of life, and eat and live forever'–Therefore the LORD God sent him out of the garden of Eden to till the ground from which he was taken,"

Genesis 3:22-23

Because of the magnitude of sin itself and the fact that Adam was created by God Himself (Adam did not proceed from a woman), in order for our sins to be forgiven, an unblemished lamb had to be sacrificed. Jesus was the unblemished Lamb of God that washes away the sins of the world. Jesus volunteered for this sacrifice and laid down His life for our salvation. That is why Jesus is the only way. We can only be saved by accepting Jesus Christ as our Lord and Savior. We can find that in the book of Romans chapter 10.

"...that if you confess with your mouth the Lord Jesus and believe in your heart that God has raised Him from the dead, you will be saved. For with the heart one believes unto righteousness, and with the mouth confession is made unto salvation."

Romans 10:9-10

If we think about it, Adam and Eve had everything their hearts desired in the garden of Eden as long as they stayed in obedience to God's commands. I like to imagine sometimes how different life would be now, if Adam and Eve didn't make such poor choice; but then again, the serpent (devil) was wise and fooled them. That explains why we humans are very gullible, easily persuaded by worldly things and worldly people. From the moment we are born (babies), we are unfortunately born with the traits of disobedience and rebellion. We see it in toddlers, pre-teens, teens, grownups, and some elderly folks too, disappointingly. We see it in the workplace, schools, home, and some churches.

The Home

How many times at home do we have to tell our children to pick up after themselves, clean the room, do their homework, brush their teeth, and so on and so forth, but our words fall on empty ears. Why? Because social media is subliminally teaching our children to be disobedient without them even knowing they are being programmed to act rebelliously to their parents. The same way, commercials or advertisements are full of subliminal messages that get in our subconscious to do what the advertisement is telling us to do. Whether it is pornography, alcohol, cigarettes, drugs, food, you name it. Be vigilant and keep your children safe and away from any form of social media or at least monitor what they do on a daily basis on the websites they visit.

The Workplace

How about the workplace? How many of us have had to train someone new (a new employee) in our lifetime? In most instances that is a very time-consuming thing, where patience is necessary to fulfill the expectations of the employer. Training someone who does not listen or follow instructions very well is a very challenging and frustrating thing, for sure. Disobedience is present everywhere in our lives, unfortunately.

School

How about school? How many times do we get calls for some things our kids are not listening to or following up on, even though we do our best at home to teach them well, to be respectful and to listen to their teachers. Well, nowadays it would be a good thing not to listen to the woke teachers' nonsense, but that will put you in the insurrectionist category. If we speak the truth, we're revolutionaries and are a "threat to democracy." Completely backwards views. The worst part is that they believe their delusions and think we don't know what they're up to, lol.

The Church

Some pastors are cracking under the pressure of the inclusion anti-God activist. They now allow same sex marriage in their churches, which is abomination in the eyes of God according to Leviticus 18:22. Pastors are now encouraging members of their churches to attend same sex ceremonies. Really? Basing it on their own view and self-approval, disobediently bypassing and ignoring the laws and commandments of the Almighty GOD.

Only wisdom comes from God, and the guidance of the Holy Spirit within us can actually help us to be obedient. Obedience to God's Word and commandments is a wonderful thing; lots of blessings will come our way and prevent us from failure when tempted, for the most part. It is all up to us, meaning that we will aways falter somehow, some way, but not in the magnitude as when we were in the world.

When we become Christians, that does not make us exempt from temptations and sinning. I have seen brothers who have taken two steps forward and on occasion ten steps backwards. Most of them, except a very small percentage, have come back. Some are still lost, and I have to try to bring them back out of the clutches of the enemy, God willing. Be supportive of each other and help each other out by confessing what is being put in your minds by the enemy.

The world is a bad place right now, and it is getting more difficult to navigate through it. The enemy's plan is well laid out and being executed by his followers, who have sold their souls for riches, fame, and self-exaltation. Please guard your children, since they are the target (mostly) of these agendas running simultaneously in the world. Always fact check things; vetting things we are being told is a good practice. Don't be deceived. Pray to the Almighty God for discernment and guidance, and to keep you from the bombardment of the enemy's temptations he is unleashing against us believers.

Dear brothers and sisters, just remember John 3:16. Stay in prayer always and read the Word of God every day.

CHAPTER THREE

LIKE IN THE DAYS OF NOAH

The story of Noah and the ark is perhaps one of the most popular stories in the Bible, not just because of the great undertaking, back in those days, to build such large floating structure like the ark. Noah was blameless and chosen by Jehovah God, along with seven other members of his family, to perpetuate humanity. God commanded Noah to build an ark in which he would house his family and every living thing of all flesh, male and female.

> *"Make yourself an ark of gopherwood; make rooms in the ark, and cover it inside and outside with pitch."*
>
> **Genesis 6:14**

> *"And behold, I myself am bringing floodwaters on the earth, to destroy from under heaven all flesh in which is the breath of life; everything that is on the earth shall die. But I will establish My covenant with*

you; and you should go into the ark – you, your sons, your wife, and your sons' wives with you. And of every living thing of all flesh you shall bring two of every sort into the ark, to keep them alive with you; they shall be male and female."

Genesis 6:17-19

Now we will devote ourselves to review the deluge in the book of Genesis, to understand why God decided to end the life of all flesh on the face of the earth. My thinking is that people in those days were living as people are living now on earth, especially here in the United States of America, Godless, selfish, violent, lost and without direction, wicked, perverted (marrying man and man and woman and woman). This is an abomination to God. (Leviticus 18:22 and Romans 1:24-27)

"You shall not lie with a male as with a woman. It is an abomination."

Leviticus 18:22

" Now it came to pass, when men began to multiply on the face of the earth, and daughters were born to them, that the sons of God saw daughters of men, that they were beautiful; and they took wives for themselves of all whom they chose. And the LORD said, 'My spirit shall not strive with man forever, for he is indeed flesh; yet his days shall be one hundred and twenty years.' There were

giants on the earth in those days, and also afterward, when the sons of God came in to the daughters of men and they bore children to them. Those were the mighty men who were of old, men of renown. Then the LORD saw that the wickedness was great in the earth, and that every intent of the thoughts of his heart was only evil continually. And the LORD was sorry that He had made man on the earth, and He was grieved in His heart. So the LORD said, 'I will destroy whom I have created from the face of the earth, both man and beast, creeping thing and birds of the air, for I am sorry that I have made them.' But Noah found grace in the eyes of the LORD."

Genesis 6:1-8

"And God said to Noah, 'The end of all flesh has come before Me, for the earth is filled with violence through them; and behold, I will destroy them with the earth.'"

Genesis 6:13

"And it came to pass after seven days that the waters of the flood were on earth. In the six hundredth year of Noah's life, in the second month, the seventeenth day of the month, on that day all the fountains of the great deep were broken up, and the windows of heaven were opened. And the rain was on the earth forty days and forty nights."

Genesis 7:10-12

"The waters prevailed fifteen cubits upward, and the mountains were covered. And all flesh died that moved on the earth: birds and cattle and beasts and every creeping thing that creeps on the earth, and every man. All in whose nostrils was the breath of the spirit of life, all that was on dry land, died. So He destroyed all living things that were on the face of the ground: both man and cattle, creeping thing and bird of the air. They were destroyed from the earth. Only Noah and those who were with him in the ark remained alive."

Genesis 7:20-23

God established a covenant with Noah and his descendants after him. God also mentions the sign of the covenant, the rainbow, which now has been hijacked by who else, the transgender movement, the one containing tons of letters. The rainbow is a holy sign, designed by God. How can something so meaningful and beautiful be polluted by something so ungodly as the transgender movement and well-funded activists? Do we need to mention who's funding this nonsense? No, not really; we know who he is. Most definitely an evil man.

"'And as for Me, behold, I establish My covenant with you and with your descendants after you, and with every living creature that is with you: the birds, the cattle, and every

beast of the earth with you, of all that go out of the ark, every beast of the earth. Thus I establish My covenant with you: never again shall all flesh be cut off by the waters of the flood; never again shall there be a flood to destroy the earth.' And God said: 'This is the sign of the covenant which I make between Me and you, and every living creature that is with you, for perpetual generations: I set My rainbow in the cloud, and it shall be for the sign of the covenant between Me and the earth.'"

Genesis 9:9-13

When a nation turns its back on God or abandons its commitment to protect Israel, most definitely it will face His wrath. I believe this has already happened to the United States of America. All you have to do is watch "regular" television. Embedded in commercials, news, movies, music, and documentaries is a hidden agenda; we don't need to be geniuses to figure this out. The agenda is to make this country atheist, violent, and perverse, starting by attacking the most vulnerable, our children. They are running part of the agenda in our school systems, introducing and forcing transgenderism and sex re-assignment, knowing very well that our sex has been already assigned by God. We know the story of Sodom and Gomorrah; they turned their back on God, and look what happened to them: destruction and complete annihilation.

In our society nowadays, we're not allowed to speak the truth, we're not allowed to make a point, dissent is prohibited and persecuted, we're not allowed to speak about God. Churches are being burnt; pastors are getting shot in the streets for preaching the Gospel of Jesus Christ. We've become a society where good is bad and bad is good. Literally, the foundation for the anti-Christ is being laid in front of our own eyes by our own so-called leaders. This same agenda is being pushed on other countries around the world; surprisingly is being accepted. Thankfully, we have strong Godly leaders in some Latin-American countries such as El Salvador's President Nayib Bukele.

What this agenda does: it alters the behavior of the people who buy into this garbage. It changes and alters their view of reality by pushing and financing drug addiction. The purpose is to make us all useless and unable to fight back for what's coming. We are going to see what the apostle Paul said about the unrighteousness of man in the book of Romans.

> *"...because, although they knew God, they did not glorify Him as God, nor were thankful, but became futile in their thoughts and their foolish hearts were darkened. Professing to be wise, they became fools, and changed the glory of the incorruptible God into an image made like corruptible man – and birds and four-footed animals and creeping things. Therefore God also gave them up to*

uncleanness, in the lusts of their hearts, to dishonor their bodies among themselves, who exchanged the truth of God for the lie, and worshiped and served the creature rather than the creator, who is blessed forever. Amen. For this reason God gave them up to vile passions. For even their women exchanged the natural use for what is against nature. Likewise also the men, leaving the natural use of the woman, burned in their lust for one another, men and men committing what is shameful, and receiving in themselves the penalty of their error which was due. And even as they did not like to retain God in their knowledge, God gave them over to a debased mind, to do those things which are not fitting; being filled with all unrighteousness, sexual immorality, wickedness, covetousness, maliciousness; full of envy, murder, strife, deceit, evil-mindedness; they are whisperers, backbiters, haters of God, violent, proud, boasters, inventors of evil things, disobedient to parents, undiscerning, untrustworthy, unloving, unforgiving, unmerciful; who, knowing the righteous judgement of God, that those who practice such things are deserving of death, not only do the same but also approve of those who practice them."

Romans 1:21-32

Well, that was a big portion of Romans chapter one, but it was necessary, I think. I believe, in my humble opinion, that these things the apostle Paul talked about in Romans 1 are exactly the things that are going on now. Society is being shaped by social media, dictating what we wear, how we talk, how we conduct ourselves and how we should address each other. School systems around the world are following the same orders. Not all the countries, though, thank God. The indoctrination of our children begins in school, from kindergarten to college, pushing the gender identity agenda, teaching homosexuality and transgenderism to our children, confusing their little minds. We are living in a Godless society, to say the least. The minute you talk about God, people want to "cancel" you. Look what happened to Tucker Carlson for telling the truth, for fact checking what the media have told us over the years.

There is more of the apostle Paul I want you to read in the book of Galatians regarding the things we should avoid like the plague.

> *"But if you are led by the Spirit, you are not under the law. Now the works of the flesh are evident, which are: adultery, fornication, uncleanness, lewdness, idolatry, sorcery, hatred, contentions, jealousy, outbursts of wrath, selfish ambitions, dissensions, heresies, envy, murders, drunkenness, revelries, and the like; of the which I tell you beforehand, just as I also told you in the past,*

that those who practice such things will not inherit the kingdom of God."
Galatians 5:18-21

Big corporations have their hands all over the execution and success of this anti-Christ agenda. This agenda is being pushed around the world. Big corporations and big pharma have now (almost) complete control of our food supply, water supply, healthcare, and even our diseases. Cures for most chronic and terminal diseases are available, not for you and me but for the elite, for the establishment.

Be vigilant, brothers and sisters, for the enemy is always prowling like a roaring lion as Peter mentioned in his first epistle. We need to stay obedient to the word of God and discern the changes in our society to make sure we are not fooled by the enemy and his agents of darkness. These days are for certain like the days in Noah's time, and we have to navigate through this time trusting and believing in the power of our Lord Jesus Christ.

"Be sober, be vigilant; because your adversary the devil walks about like a roaring lion, seeking whom he may devour."
1 Peter 5:8

Stay in prayer always. Amen.

CHAPTER FOUR

THE DEITY OF CHRIST

I want to talk about a controversial subject that lingers between religions, denominations, and churches. That is, the deity of our Lord Jesus Christ. What I understand from the scriptures is that Jesus sits to the right side of the throne of God.

A few religions believe that Jesus was simply a prophet. Some believe He is, or was, an apostle. Typically, the religions or cults who believe this are not reading the true scriptures. Usually, they print their own Bibles, much different than the true scriptures. In some of their "Bibles" they omit lots of soul-saving messages to make you believe in who their main focus is, most likely another human being, who claims to talk to God, or had "visions" of the leader or founder of their church being divine, or as equal to, or close to be like Christ. This is heresy, evil to the core. There's a so-called pastor who claims God asked for his opinion, really!!! Blasphemer. I loved what Justin Peters had to say about this lost soul's nonsense: "And he who thinks he can counsel God is a fool." *(233 Justin Peters:*

Dangerous Doctrines). There are so many of these fools misleading lots and lots of people, therefore, brothers and sisters, like the Bereans, make it a daily practice to read the scriptures, so if you know someone going to these churches, you can shine the light of truth upon them. Because if they are preaching a differing Jesus in these churches, they are preaching a different gospel.

On several occasions Jesus said that if we have seen Him, we've seen the Father. What I understand about this statement is that Jesus is God, as God the Father is, and God the Holy Spirit is. I want to list some verses from the Gospels and from the book of Genesis in the Old Testament. The first thing I want you to notice is what God said in Genesis 1:26 before creating man. God said, " *Let Us.* " So, this tells me that God wasn't alone during the creation of the world, especially on the fifth day, when He created man. Interestingly, Jesus told us that, in John 17:5.

> *"Then God said, 'Let Us make man in Our image, according to Our likeness; let them have dominion over the fish of the sea, over the birds of the air, and over the cattle, over all the earth and over every creeping thing that creeps on the earth.'"*
>
> **Genesis 1:26**

> *"And now, O Father, glorify Me together with Yourself, with the glory which I had with You before the world was."*
>
> **John 17:5**

This is evidence that Jesus was involved in the creation of the world or it was created by Him as John states in the beginning of his Gospel.

> *"In the beginning was the Word, and the Word was with God, and the Word was God. He was in the beginning with God. All things were made through Him, and without Him nothing was made that was made."*
> **John 1:1-3**

Some might wonder what or who is the Word, or how do we know Jesus is the Word referred by John. To corroborate this, we need to go further into John's gospel.

> *"And the Word became flesh and dwelt among us, and we beheld His glory, the glory as of the only begotten of the Father, full of grace and truth."*
> **John 1:14**

It is clear that the Word is Jesus Christ, and that He is God in the flesh. There are many instances when Jesus makes reference to His authority to forgive sins here on earth. Many times, when He healed people, He would say, "Your sins are forgiven." In the book of Mathew Jesus said this:

> *"Then behold, they brought to Him a paralytic lying on a bed. When Jesus saw their faith, He said to the paralytic, 'Son, be of good cheer;*

your sins are forgiven you.' And at once some of the scribes said within themselves, 'This man blasphemes!' But Jesus, knowing their thoughts, said, 'Why do you think evil in your hearts? For which is easier, to say, "your sins are forgiven you," or to say, "Arise and walk'"? But that you may know that the Son of Man has power on earth to forgive sins' – then He said to the paralytic, 'Arise, take up your bed, and go to your house.'"

Matthew 9:2-6

We know that Jesus is God in the flesh, fully (divine) God and fully (human) Man; there's no way anyone can deny it or even try to do so. The dispute going on between faiths, denominations, or religions around the world regarding the deity of Jesus is actually senseless. If we are to interpret the scriptures, we need to pray to God to give us discernment, so that when we teach or simply share the Gospel of Jesus with others, we do it as accurately as possible and not share an incorrect or diluted version of the Gospel. We need to fact check what we are being taught, whether the teaching comes from family, friends, or your own pastor. Open the scriptures yourself and pray to God to let His Holy Spirit guide you in the journey. Learn from the Bereans, mentioned in the book of Acts, chapter 17. We should be like them, fact checking what we are told and searching the scriptures daily. Not only the scriptures, but any information coming our way that might jeopardize our salvation, our lives, our health, and our finances.

"Then the brethren immediately sent Paul and Silas away by night to Berea. When they arrived, they went into the synagogue of the Jews. These were more fair-minded than those in Thessalonica, in that they received the word with all readiness, and searched the scriptures daily to find out whether these things were so."

Acts 17:10-11

From the Bereans we have learned a very important practice, which is check the scriptures daily. That way, when someone tells us things such as Jesus wasn't God, we can educate them about the truth and show them the scriptures. Hopefully, they will be open-minded and susceptible to persuasion. As Christians, we need to do our part, just like when we work a job, we have to do the tasks assigned to us. The life of a Christian is the same way. Our job is to study the scriptures daily and proclaim the Gospel of Jesus Christ boldly and without fear.

I do not want to mislead anyone or send them through the wide door, the one door Jesus mentioned here:

"Enter by the narrow gate; for wide is the gate and broad is the way that leads to destruction, and there many who go in by it. Because narrow is the gate and difficult is the way which leads to life, and there are few who find it."

Matthew 7:13-14

Jesus is the Son of man, the Son of God, He is God in the flesh, who sits to the right side of the glory of God in the Holy of Holies, the one who was there in the beginning of creation. Let us not forget that Jesus is God in the flesh, who gave His life for the salvation of the world and shed His holy blood.

Following is another passage in the Bible that helps us confirm the deity of Jesus and that he was in heaven before coming to earth::

> *"When He had come to the other side, to the country of the Gergesenes, there met Him two demon-possessed men, coming out of the tombs, exceedingly fierce, so that no one could pass that way. And suddenly they cried out, saying, 'What have we to do with You, Jesus, You Son of God? Have you come here to torment us before the time?' Now a good way off from them there was a herd of many swine feeding. So the demons begged Him, saying, 'If You cast us out, permit us to go away into the herd of swine.' And He said to them, 'Go.' So when they had come out, they went into the herd of swine. And suddenly the whole herd of swine ran violently down the steep place into the sea, and perished in the water."*
> **Matthew 8:28-32**

Well, if Jesus was just a man or a prophet, why did these demons recognize Him and call Him the Son of God? Furthermore, why would Jesus have the authority to torment any demon in the invisible realm if He is not God? The demons knew who He was and called Him by name. If Jesus was just a prophet like some religions (cults) believe or claim, why did the demons know Him and obey Him?

People who are preaching such things as Jesus is not God to their congregation are false prophets and are misleading many, sending people to hell. It is our duty as Christians to help these people as much as we can, so they can know the truth, be saved, and find the way to heaven, which is only found through Jesus Christ, our Lord and Savior.

We will study false prophets in the next chapter, because pastors like these are false prophets. They don't proclaim the true Gospel of Jesus Christ, but a diluted version of it, omitting the truth. Some paint their truth as happy, prosperous, wealthy, no worries, good health, and prosperity in the world, when the fact is that the true church will be persecuted, chastised, and executed. We, the true church, have a very grim future, as mentioned below:

> *"Yes, and all who desire to live Godly in Christ Jesus will suffer persecution. But evil men and impostors will grow worse and worse, deceiving and being deceived."*

Timothy 3:12-13

"Blessed are those who are persecuted for righteousness' sake, For theirs is the kingdom of heaven. Blessed are you when they revile and persecute you and say all kind of evil against you falsely for My sake."

Matthew 5:10-11

"If the world hates you, you know that it hated Me before it hated you. If you were of the world, the world will love its own. Yet because you are not of the world, but I chose you out of the world, therefore the world hates you."

John 15:18-19

In this book I have used the New King James Version of the Bible, to make it easier for new Christians or anyone that struggles with understanding the King James Version. This especially applies to people like me, whose first language is not English, lol. But by all means, please feel free to use a good Bible translation , such as the King James Version. Some versions omit words which do not change the message, such as the version I am using, but contemporary language translations can be more explanatory and understandable than other versions.

Don't let the enemy confuse you and make you believe that Jesus is just a prophet or just a human being who had God's blessings. Help each other out, brothers and sisters, in understanding the scriptures. The devil can confuse our minds and distract us from our responsibilities, duties, and goals as a Christian. Stay in prayer always; that works for me when I am being tempted. I immediately get on my knees and pray to God for help against my temptations, and He will deliver me. I do fall into temptations every once in a while, but I can attest to what God does for me when I pray not to let the enemy tempt me.

In any case, don't let anyone tell you that Jesus is not God in the flesh. I believe I have presented enough evidence to support the claim that Jesus is God. No one else in the Bible has shown authority over demons, who, by the way know Him (Jesus) by name. If anyone preaches to you something different than what's written in the scriptures, run away fast.

He is the Alpha and the Omega, the beginning and the end, the first and the last. Amen.

CHAPTER FIVE

FALSE PROPHETS

This is one fascinating subject because there are so many false prophets nowadays. It is hard to believe, but all this was mentioned in the Bible several times. To a Christian it is not a surprise, because it was expected. The most astonishing thing is to see how many people are falling for these doctrines and following these so-called "pastors." Another observation is how many women are getting involved in ministry, most of them are married to the false teacher or shall we say prosperity preacher or motivational speaker which should never be called "pastors." We'll see later in the chapter what the scriptures have to say about women in ministry. We'll start, however, with the false preachers and their agenda. We've been warned about these end times days by our Lord Jesus Christ and some of His apostles. Let's start with what Jesus had to say about the end times and the false prophets who will rise, in Mathew 24.

"Now as He sat on the mount of olives, the disciples came to Him privately, saying, 'Tell

*us, when will these things be? And what will
be the sign of Your coming, and of the end
of the age?' And Jesus answered and said to
them: 'Take heed that no one deceives you,
for many will come in My name, saying, "I
am the Christ;" and will deceive many.'"*

Matthew 24:3-5

*"Then many false prophets will rise up and
deceive many."*

Matthew 24:11

If we stop and analyze with discernment what Jesus
said in the book of Mathew, chapter 24, we'll get to the
conclusion that we are actually living in the end times,
given the number of false prophets who have already been
raised up. We are going to read what the apostle Paul said
about false prophets. In addition, we will see what the
books of Timothy, Peter, John, Galatians, and Jude had to
say about the false prophets, the apostasy of the end days
and much more.

*"But I fear, lest somehow, as the serpent
deceived Eve by his craftiness, so your minds
may be corrupted from the simplicity that
is in Christ. For if he who comes preaches
another Jesus whom we have not preached,
or if you receive a different spirit which you
have not received, or a different gospel which
you have not accepted – you may well put up
with it."*

2 Corinthians 11:3-4

"Now the Spirit expressly says that in latter times some will depart from the faith, giving heed to deceiving spirits and doctrines of demons, speaking lies in hypocrisy, having their own conscience seared with a hot iron, forbidding to marry, and commending to abstain from foods which God created to be received with thanksgiving by those who believe and know the truth."

1 Timothy 4:1-3

"But there were also false prophets among the people, even as there will be false teachers among you, who will secretly bring in destructive heresies, even denying the Lord who brought them, and bring on themselves swift destruction. And many will follow their destructive ways, because of whom the way of truth will be blasphemed. By covetousness they will exploit you with deceptive words; for a long time their judgement has not been idle, and their destruction does not slumber."

2 Peter 2:1-3

"Little children, it is the last hour; and as you have heard that the antichrist is coming, even now many antichrists have come, by which we know that it is the last hour."

1 John 2:18

"Beloved, while I was very diligent to write to you concerning our common salvation, I

found it necessary to write to you exhorting you to contend earnestly for the faith which was once for all delivered to the saints. For certain men have crept in unnoticed, who long ago were marked out for this condemnation, ungodly men, who turn the grace of our God into lewdness and deny the only Lord God and our Lord Jesus Christ."

Jude 1:3-4

"I marvel that you are turning away so soon from Him who called you in the grace of Christ, to a different gospel, which is not another; but there are some who trouble you and want to prevent the gospel of Christ."

Galatians 1:6-7

It is imperative, in my humble opinion, that new Christians understand how critical these times are. It is time to search the scriptures and pray to God for discernment, wisdom, humility, empathy, understanding, and courage for what's coming, so we're not caught doing ungodly things.

People are being misled by megachurches whose pastors are preaching an incorrect version of the gospel, or preaching a completely different gospel, or a diluted version of it. The main topic in these churches is prosperity, wealth, health, happiness, while they're getting filthy rich from tithes from making people feel good about themselves, completely opposite of what our Lord Jesus Christ told the apostles about the responsibility of preaching the gospel.

He certainly didn't tell His apostles to own the latest ship to travel in, to have three or four multi-million-dollar homes, or to be comfortable in the best beds money can buy. Let's see what Jesus said regarding these topics:

> *" 'No one can serve two masters; for either he*
> *will hate the one and love the other, or else he*
> *will be loyal to the one, and despise the other.*
> *You cannot serve God and mammon. '"*
> **Matthew 6:24**

Note: In other versions of the Bible, the word mammon is substituted with the word "money" or "riches" in the verse above. In the verses below, in some Bibles, the word rust is substituted with the word "urine"

We know where the hearts of these prosperity pastor are: *on the world (or hell), not in heaven.* The problem is that they are taking their followers or congregation with them, straight to hell, and their followers are not even aware of it.

> *" 'Do not lay up for yourselves treasures*
> *on earth, where moth and rust destroy and*
> *where thieves break in and steal; but lay up*
> *for yourselves treasures in heaven, where*
> *neither moth nor rust destroys and where*
> *thieves do not break in and steal. For where*
> *your treasure is, there your heart will be*
> *also. '"*
> **Matthew 6:19-21**

> *"And when Jesus saw great multitudes about Him, He gave a command to depart to the other side. Then a certain scribe came and said to Him, 'Teacher, I will follow you wherever you go.' 20 And Jesus said to him, 'Foxes have holes and birds of the air have nests, but the Son of Man has nowhere to lay His head.'"*
>
> **Matthew 8:18-20**

The Son of Man had nowhere to lay His head, so why do these prosperity teaching "preachers" feel so entitled to own two, three, or four houses through the sweat of their congregation who they're dragging with them to hell? The Son of Man, who, by the way, is God in the flesh, humbled Himself and lived and served like a poor human being. So, why do these false pastors want to live like kings? Simple: because their father the devil is the king of this world, for now, and they (the false teachers) feel compelled to live by his standards.

Let's see what Jesus said to a rich young man who wanted to know how to have eternal life:

> *"Now behold, one came and said to Him, 'Good Teacher, what good thing shall I do that I may have eternal life?' So he said to him, 'Why do you call Me good? No one is good but One, that is, God. But if you want to enter into life, keep the commandments.' He said to Him, 'Which ones?' Jesus said,*

'You shall not murder, 'You shall not commit adultery,'" "'You shall not steal." "'You shall not bear false witness."' "'Honor your father and your mother,'" and 'You shall love your neighbor as yourself.'" The young man said to Him, 'All these things I have kept from my youth. What do I still lack?' Jesus said to him, 'If you want to be perfect, go, sell what you have and give it to the poor, and you will have treasures in heaven; and come, follow me.'"

Matthew 19:16-21

"Then Jesus said to His disciples, 'Assuredly, I say to you that it is hard for a rich man to enter the kingdom of heaven. And again I say to you, it is easier for a camel to go through the eye of a needle than for a rich man to enter the kingdom of God.'"

Matthew 19:23-24

There's one more thing in the scriptures that I want to show you which is relevant to this subject and to the existence of hell as a real place. We'll find this in the book of Luke.

"There was a certain rich man who was clothed in purple and fine linen and fared sumptuously every day. But there was a certain beggar named Lazarus, full of sores, who was laid at his gate, desiring to be fed

with the crumbs which fell from the rich man's table. Moreover the dogs came and licked his sores. So it was that the beggar died, and was carried by the angels to Abraham's bosom. The rich man also died and was buried. And being in torments in Hades, he lifted up his eyes and saw Abraham afar off, and Lazarus in his bosom. Then he cried and said, 'Father Abraham, have mercy on me, and send Lazarus that he may dip the tip of his finger in water and cool my tongue; for I am tormented in this flame.' But Abraham said, 'Son, remember that in your lifetime you received your good things, and likewise Lazarus evil things; but now he is comforted and you are tormented. And besides all this, between us and you there is a great gulf fixed, so that those who want to pass from here to you cannot, nor can those from there pass to us.' Then he said, 'I beg you therefore, father, that you would send him to my father's house, for I have five brothers, that he may testify to them, lest they also come to this place of torment.' Abraham said to him, 'They have Moses and the prophets; let them hear them.' And he said, 'No, father Abraham; but if one goes to them from the dead, they will repent.' But he said to him, 'If they do not hear Moses and the prophets, neither will they be persuaded though one rise from the dead.'"

Luke 16:19-31

Women Preaching the Gospel

The other subject we are going to review based on scriptures, is women's roles in the church, as I mentioned in the beginning of this chapter. I know this is going to be a hot topic, and hard to accept for some women. It is nothing personal; I am just pointing out what the scriptures say about this subject. Basing everything on the scriptures, if women are preaching in churches, should they be considered false teachers? I don't know; I have seen prominent preachers talk about this subject during their services. The true gospel preachers definitely disagree with women preaching, based on scriptures. But there are others who approve this practice, most of these preachers are related to these women, many of whom are married to the "pastor" who will allow them to preach, as if that call is up to them. The apostle Paul in his letters mentioned this trend going on in the churches he visited. He gave stern directions to the leaders of the churches regarding the role of women in the house of God. Let's review all the apostles Paul and Peter had to say about this matter.

> *"For God is not the author of confusion but of peace, as in all the churches of the saints. Let your women keep silent in the churches, for they are not permitted to speak; but they are to be submissive, as the law also says. And if they want to learn something, let them ask their own husbands at home; for it is*

shameful for women to speak in church."
1 Corinthians 14:33-35

"Wives, submit to your own husbands, as to the Lord. For the husband is the head of the wife, as also Christ is head of the church; and He is the Savior of the body."
Ephesians 5:22-23

"Let the woman learn in silence with all submission. And I do not permit a woman to teach or to have authority over a man, but to be in silence."
1 Timothy 2:11-12

"Beloved, I now write to you this second epistle (in both of which I stir up your pure minds by way of reminder), That you may be mindful be mindful of the words which were spoken before by the holy prophets, and of the commandments of us, the apostles of the Lord and Savior, Knowing the first: that scoffers will come in the last days, walking according to their own lusts, and saying, 'Where is the promise of His coming? For since the fathers fell asleep, all things continue as they were from the beginning of creation.'"
(2 Peter 3:1-4)

It is very clear what is mentioned in the scriptures regarding women preaching. It can be proven very easily as we just read the verses above. There are a few great pastors out there preaching regarding this growing issue. I really don't like to mention people's names; however, when it is something of importance in these days it is very worth it; there should not be an issue. John McArthur, one of my favorite pastors, and Voddie Baucham (another favorite of mine) both agree regarding this issue; that women do not belong in front of a church's pulpit.

Since I mention some of my favorite pastors, I don't want to leave other favorites out, lol. God bless them for the extraordinary work they do on a daily basis lol.

Here they are: John McArthur, Justin Peters, Allen Jackson, Tony Evans, Jack Hibbs, Robert Jeffress, John Hagee, Phillip De Corsey, Dr. David Jeremiah, Charles Stanley, Rabi Kirk Schneider and others.

God bless all who are reading these references to the scriptures in this book.

CHAPTER SIX

TEMPTATIONS

This is a very broad subject since temptations come from all directions, and in many different forms and delivery methods. Directions: from work, family, friends, church, social media, and the internet. Different forms: lust, drunkenness, drugs, thievery, conflicts, gambling, etc. Delivery methods: social media, phone calls (with links, sometimes), in person conversations, texts, emails.

Let's look at the different forms of temptation; lust, for instance, can have a tremendous impact in the lives of a family. Yes, family; when there's adultery, the whole family is affected, starting with the lies to the spouse, who most of the time is clueless as to what's going on. This is thanks to the sophistication of technology, including silent texting or other forms of messaging. The moment the spouse finds out about the affair, things change. The interaction between husband and wife becomes hostile and conflictive. Children have to witness that and wonder if the argument is because of something they have done wrong. Jesus and His apostles had a few things to say about this subject. Let's look at what the apostle Paul had to say in 1 Corinthians 6:9-11.

> *"Do you not know that the unrighteous will not inherit the kingdom of God? Do not be deceived. Neither fornicators, nor idolaters,* **nor adulterers,** *nor homosexuals, nor sodomites, nor thieves, nor covetous, nor drunkards, nor revilers, nor extortioners will inherit the kingdom of God. And such were some of you. But you were washed, but you were sanctified, but you were justified, in the name of our Lord Jesus, and by the spirit of our God."*

Let us review all the things the apostle Paul said about the unrighteous not inheriting the Kingdom of God (above). Besides adultery, we will review other bad traits that are the consequence of temptations. Let's do it in the order the apostle Paul presented them.

fornicators

Fornicators, in my opinion, are those tempted and looking for a one night stand every time they go out to the bars with their socalled "friends." In their minds, no one will know or find out, but God knows everything. He sees everything we do, hear, or say. However, these individuals follow through with the temptation. The sad part is that women are just as bad as men nowadays.

Idolaters

We can go on and on with this subject, but we will see what the main and most prominent form of idolatry is. Just for your self-awareness, if you don't know your Ten Commandments, idolatry is extremely offensive to our God, such that His first and second commandments for us to follow state the following, in both Exodus and Deuteronomy.

> *"You shall have no other gods before Me."*
> **Exodus 20:3**

> *"You shall not make for yourself a carved image- any likeness of anything that is in heaven above, or that is in the earth beneath, or that is in the water under the earth; you shall not bow down to them. For I the Lord your God, am a jealous God, visiting the iniquity of the fathers upon the children of the third and fourth generations of those who hate Me, but showing mercy to thousands, to those who love Me and keep My commandments."*
> **Exodus 20:4**

Well, this tells us that our God is a jealous God. He wants the worship of His people and the people who love Him and put Him above all things. God should be the first thought in our minds before starting anything, such as endeavors, businesses, waking up, and as much as possible in our daily thoughts.

Adulterers

These may be long term relationships for the most part, or they can be off and on relationships while being married. In any case, it is a sin and against the seventh commandment. Adultery can never end well, most of the time. It causes a lot of hurt or/and pain if the other party is completely committed to the marriage, and first of all, in love. First, let us read the Word of God regarding adultery in His Ten Commandments (Exodus 20:14), and what Jesus had to say about adultery in the book of Mathew, and the apostle Paul in the book of Galatians.

"You shall not commit adultery."
Exodus 20:14

"You have heard that it was said to those of old, 'you should not commit adultery'. But I say to you that whoever looks at a woman to lust for her has already committed adultery with her in his heart."
Matthew 5:27-28

"Now the works of the flesh are evident, which are: adultery, fornication, uncleanness, lewdness,"
Galatians 5:19

Homosexuals

Interesting subject for these times, lol; who hasn't heard of the "lgb????" cult or whatever that is or means. I'm not well informed about what it is, nor do I want to be; all I know is what God says about same sex relationships. As far as I know, sexual relationships with the same sex or gender are an abomination to God. Let's see what the scriptures have to say about this subject in Leviticus chapter 18, when God gave Moses the laws of sexual morality.

> *"You shall not lie with a male as with a woman. It is an abomination."*
> **Leviticus 18:22**

I don't think we can add anything to this subject. It is clearly an abomination to God. Just keep in mind that God loves every human being, He just does not like the acts, He hates the acts, that's exactly why He sent His Son Jesus to earth to die for our sins and be redeemed through His blood.

Sodomites

This subject can be a little tricky, because of the fact that in our times, the term sodomite means someone who practices sodomy. Kind of goes along with the previous subject. It could be a term that was based on the practices that took place in the city of Sodom, which was destroyed. I suppose if someone practices the rituals that were practiced

71

in Sodom, they can be considered a Sodomite. I think all this is subjective. I could not find a clear definition of the word or label sodomite. However, it seems like it is related to the immoralities that took place in Sodom, which led to its destruction.

Thieves

Wow, this is a broad subject if we include governments, lol. Well, thievery comes in many forms, some of them we don't even realize. For instance, do you know you can steal time? Yes, when we work in a place and you are told you only have fifteen minutes for a break and you take thirty minutes, you stole fifteen minutes of time. So, whatever you earn in fifteen minutes, that's what you stole from your employer. One of Jesus' twelve apostles was a thief. Did you know that? We can find this in John 12:4-6.

> *"But one of His disciples, Judas Iscariot, Simon's son, who would betray Him, said, " Why was this fragrant oil not sold for three hundred denarii and given to the poor?" This he said, not that he cared for the poor, but because he was a thief, and he had the money box; and he used to take what was put in it."*

In addition to this, not stealing is part of the Ten Commandments, commandment number eight. You can find it in Exodus 20:15.

"You shall not steal."

Other types of theft are not paying back a loan, taking what does not belong to you, borrowing things from work and not returning them, robbing a bank, taking things from grocery stores without paying for them, etc. Temptations make us do a lot of things that do not align with God's expectations of us. In many cases, people succumb to all or most of these negative behaviors, unfortunately.

Covetous

Basically, this can be called envy. We see this issue more and more with individuals desiring someone else's wife, cars, houses, you name it. Have you seen that popular bumper sticker? "The one with the most toys wins." Wins what? Debt? Disappointments? Emptiness? Unfortunately, it is a reality. These individuals serve a different God; things/possessions are their God. People kill just to get someone else's things, money, cars, you name it. It happens in this world ruled by the enemy, who dazzles the ungodly with riches, fame, or whatever they're desiring or looking for, but for a price: their souls. Most people with these issues are not Godly and perhaps not attending church, for sure.

In addition, God commands us not to covet in His Ten Commandments, number ten. We can find it on the book of Exodus 20:17.

*"You shall not covet your neighbor's house;
you shall not covet your neighbor's wife, nor
his male servant, nor his female servant, nor
his ox, nor his donkey, nor anything that is
your neighbor's."*

The life of a true Christian may seem boring to some, but when you love God and Jesus Christ, every day is an adventure, searching for ways to serve our God, following Jesus' teachings and letting Him make a residence in your heart. Worldly things are the least in a Christian's priorities. Once you deny yourself, your world view is different. We will begin to see where we can make a positive impact, whether we help a family member or a complete stranger.

Drunkards

Drunkenness is a bad thing. Like lust, it destroys the family, it destroys friendships, it affects work and the safety of oneself and that of others. According to research, the statistics for death for drunk driving crashes are roughly around 37 people per day. That's one person every 39 minutes. In addition, drinking can lead to some really bad diseases, such as: cancer, liver disease, diabetes, esophagus/mouth cancer, etc. Alcohol is very destructive for the human body.

The agenda is to divide the family nucleus and take over the life of our children to alter their perspective on the truth about life, but first and foremost is to take God away from every home, school, and all institutions in the world. The father of all lies is working hard to mislead and steal any future Christians from God.

Revilers

This is referred to a person who's abusive in language, stemming from anger or hatred. Well, we can actually think of road rage as an example of revilers. Have you ever cut off someone on the road by mistake? Yes, some people get so crazy about innocent stuff that happens on the road, sometimes they pull guns, knives, or machetes on people.

We can also see that in the workplace. The world is full of angry people nowadays. Even Christians preaching on the streets get attacked for no reason. Just for telling the audience what God says about what they're doing. Just for reading the scriptures to the people of the world.

Recently, a preacher was shot in the head in Glendale, Arizona. Hans Schmidt is a miracle of God, who delivered him from the grip of death. He is recovering now but he still needs our prayers. God bless you, brother.

Extortioners

These kinds of people are very dangerous. Extortioners use force or threats to get money from innocent victims. In some countries, they have well-organized gangs that operate not just within the borders of their own countries but have expanded abroad. They are now active in many countries and even involve in kidnappings, which is the worst form of torture to a family.

There are so many ways to extort a person or a family. I'm sure you all have experienced weird phone calls telling you a nephew or a family member is in jail and needs money, or is in the hospital and needs money for medicine. People are pulling so many scams to get money of the gullible. Another good one is the credit card scam, telling people they have a payment due, and it has to be paid immediately. How about the Amazon account scam lol, telling people they have an outstanding balance and need pay immediately. That's the dangerous world we are living in.

With all that said, we have seen the explanations for what the apostle Paul was saying regarding those who will not inherit the kingdom of God, in 1 Corinthians 6:9-11.

God bless you, brothers and sisters, and stay in prayer.

CHAPTER SEVEN

PROCLAIMING THE GOSPEL OF JESUS CHRIST

As Christians, we have the obligation to proclaim the gospel of our Lord Jesus Christ to the world, including family, friends, co-workers, and all people who are receptive and have the desire to know God and His Son Jesus Christ. In my humble opinion, given the times, it is imperative that we stand up for the truth, which is that the only way to be saved is through Jesus Christ. We know that by doing that, we will be putting ourselves at risk or danger, for the simple fact that our society is anti-God, anti-truth, anti-Christ, and anti-Christians. Our faith and knowledge of the truth have been politicized. And for sure, the church is under attack. For those who still do not know (which are few), the persecution of the church has already begun here in the United States of America. In the nation once admired by many countries around the world for being the land of the free, now imprisonment and socialism are being disguised as freedom. As one of my favorite preachers, John Hagee, describes socialism: "Socialism is communism with lipstick." Very true.

Have you heard the expression "divide and conquer"? Well, that's Satan's strategy with everything. Starting in the garden of Eden, he divided men from God. If you want to conquer a country, which is what superpowers do, you trick their people into fighting with each other, killing their own brothers and sisters. It is very demonic, to the core. Then, they support both sides, for a price, money. If there's no money, they will take the countries' resources, if they cannot pay for the support given in arms and equipment to be able to defend themselves from their own brothers and sisters. What a scam. Why do you think they are superpowers? Remember, Satan does not want any human being to make it to heaven, and he is calling the shots for most of these superpowers to do what they do.

We will get in a lot of trouble in the days ahead, simply for proclaiming the truth. The enemy is a supernatural creature full of knowledge, especially when it comes to human weaknesses. He is the prince of darkness, so he would like all of us humans to be in darkness with him, because he hates us. His goal is to take over the most powerful nation on earth. Why? Because it is a role model for the world, supposedly; everything that comes out of that nation is followed or emulated by other nation's populations. He will then try to infiltrate God's churches, because they are the beacons of light upholding the moral standards of a nation. If the church of the true God gets infiltrated, then the takeover will be easy, except for those of us who know the truth and know what is coming and are blessed with discernment given to us by the Holy Spirit of God. Next, he already created division in the family, in the churches, and in the nation, creating conflict between them. "Divide and conquer," remember. Next, probably infiltrate the education system. This happened when I was going to college, that's why I quit and never finished, despite being so close. Once the conflict among ourselves in the family, churches, schools, and country is set in motion, it is nearly impossible for us to come out of it. We as a nation have lost or are losing our way, but nothing is impossible for God Almighty. Next will be the judicial system, to imprison all those who opposed this nonsensical agenda, and to free the criminals, to keep assaulting the regular hard-working men and women of this country. The medical system was infiltrated a long time ago, turning it from an institution created to serve and care for the wellbeing and good health of the population into a "cash cow" big business enterprise.

I would like to break this down even more:

Taking over a country

Satan will begin by buying politicians to serve his agenda. After getting politicians in his pocket (from many countries probably), then he will begin to take over the entertainment systems of the country, mostly TV and radio, bypassing the norms or regulations instituted or established by governments as guidelines of what is permitted to broadcast and what is not. He will target morality, by giving wider boundaries to the movie and television industries. He will proceed by starting to show ungodly things on TV such as pornography, nudity, foul language, etc. The enemy has gone as far as pushing drugs on our youth, even fomented by our own government. This will be followed by taking over the news broadcasting networks (already happened), dictating what they can and cannot say to make his agenda as natural and normal as possible. Controlling the television, radio, and movie industries, he can promote alcoholism, drug addiction and an anti-God agenda.

At least ninety to ninety-five percent of the news we see on most of the channels is fake. Broadcasters or anchors follow the same script, even to the words or sentences. It is hilarious that some people don't see it, or choose to ignore it, trusting this twisted view of woke culture. There are some, maybe a couple of television channels out there, broadcasting the truth. We as Christians need to proclaim and broadcast the gospel of Jesus Christ; it is our duty. Newspapers and magazines are no better, full of hatred for righteous and God-fearing people, or anyone that does not align with their twisted views.

The Takeover of the Church

This is actually happening as we speak. It is not a complete takeover yet, but an attempt. Lots of churches have gone woke, doing things that are against God, just to appease their critics and to satisfy the woke inclusive agenda. In January 2024, the Catholic Church started to bless homosexual couples (although not marry them), completely ignoring what God had said in the book of Leviticus 18:22. This is complete abomination in God's eyes. No man can change the things God has commanded us not to do.

Some pastors are also going woke. There's a pastor who I respect very much to this day; however, recently he gave a very controversial advice to one woman he was counselling regarding an LGBTIQ wedding: suggesting that she attend the wedding and buying them a gift. It is heart breaking to see this kind of situation, especially when involves someone well respected, who was believed to have a solid and firm foundation that will not cave under any pressure of the world. But anyway, he will be in my prayers.

In Latin America, the inclusion movement has been actively trying to infiltrate most of the countries; however, most of the countries in the region are populated by true Christians, God fearing followers of Jesus. They hit a brick wall in some countries, especially in El Salvador, where the great president of that country rejected this indoctrination of the youth; furthermore, he ordered to remove inclusion literacy from all the schools in the country. President Bukele is a Godly man who gives the glory to God for his successful leadership and for turning that country around, from being the murder capital of the world, to the safest country in the western hemisphere. He will not allow the infiltration of the church, government, schools, colleges, health systems, and family bonds, I hope.

On September 14 and 15 of 2022, in Kazakhstan, the VIIth Congress of the leaders of world and traditional religions took place .Research it; it is very interesting. The purpose of the meeting is, supposedly, for the Catholic Church and Islam to co-exist. However, when you start hearing the discussions and arguments, you are lead to believe that this is just one more motion toward one world religion. Another curious thing is, why are world leaders and international organizations involved in this meeting? To dictate to these religions the one world religion agenda? Interesting! Sounds like they are building the foundation for the anti-Christ to emerge. We, the true Christians, are being isolated because we don't go along with the nonsense going on in the world. That will put a big target on us, the true believers. They are claiming that the goal of the meeting is to achieve *peace and security* in the world. Let us see what the apostle Paul said about that.

> *"But concerning the times and the seasons, brethren, you have no need that I should write to you. For you yourselves know that the day of the Lord so comes as a thief in the night. For when they say, 'Peace and safety!' then sudden destruction comes upon them, as labor pains upon a pregnant woman."*
> **1 Thessalonians 5:1-3**

So, let's keep on eye on the progress of uniting all the religions of the world. The end game, as most of you know, is to create a one world government, one world currency, and one world religion. How do we know that? From Revelation 13 and Daniel 7, we can deduce that the anti-Christ is the world ruler, that the only currency is the mark of the beast, and that the only religion is worship of the anti-Christ himself. He wants to be worshipped by the world. Revelation 13 actually describes the one world government, one world currency, and one world religion. Let's look at what it has to say:

One World Government, One World Religion, and One World Currency

"Then I saw another beast coming up out of the earth, and he had two horns like a lamb and spoke like a dragon. And he exercises all the authority of the first beast in his presence, and causes the earth and those who dwell in it to worship the first beast, whose deadly wound was healed. He performs great signs, so that he even makes fire come down from heaven on the earth in the sight of men. And he deceives those who dwell on the earth to make an image to the beast who was wounded by the sword and lived. He was

granted power to give breath to the image of the beast, that the image of the beast should both speak and cause as many as would not worship the image of the beast to be killed. He causes all, both small and great, rich and poor, free and slave, to receive a mark on their right hand or on their foreheads, and that no one may buy or sell except one who has the mark or the name of the beast, or the number of his name. Here is wisdom. Let him who has understanding calculate the number of the beast, for is the number of a man: His number is 666."

Revelation 13:11-18

This section of Revelation sums it all up. As I always encourage you, pray to God for discernment and understanding of the scriptures. The book of Revelation can be intimidating and confusing at times, but with the power of the Holy Spirit, we can come to understand what we read.

The Takeover of the family

Well, we have already touched on this subject in other chapters, but a recap is not a bad idea. We know the worst mind-controlling tool of the enemy is social media, in addition to television, music, video games and other things that perhaps I'm not aware of. Not to mention school "friends." neighbors, and other forms of interactions. In addition to all these negative ways of losing your children, now the government actually wants to make decisions on what's best for your children. If you disagree, then you are an insurrectionist; go figure. It'll be a cold day in hell before I let the government dictate to me how to raise my own children.

The Takeover of the Schools

In most schools, our children are being indoctrinated with satanic ideologies that can make you drop to your knees and ask God why this is going on. If you look at the books the poor kids are reading, your jaw will drop. Transgenderism hour, sex reassignment, inclusion, and who knows how many other evil and satanic ideologies are being pushed into their little minds. Today, children do not need consent or permission from the parents if they want to have sex re-assignment, which includes surgery. We are literally being systematically imprisoned in our own homes and by our own government. In some schools, children are no longer allowed to say the pledge of allegiance, sing the national anthem, or pray to God.

The Takeover of the Judicial System

Well, this is a very broad subject. We see it every day on the mainstream media; on television "all channels are following a script." Attacking innocent people, just for exercising their first or second amendment rights. It seems like freedom of speech only refers to the media. You and I cannot speak the truth without suffering repercussions. Sectors or groups of the population in the United States are being isolated, targeted, and literally persecuted for believing in things that made this nation great (which no longer is, as of 2020) such as patriotism, faith, and freedom of speech. However, let's face it, there has never been such a thing as freedom, there is no such thing as democracy; let's get it through our heads. The human race has been enslaved under the banner of "democracy and human rights" for decades, if not centuries.

There are two sets of rules here in America, one for the corrupt and one for the population who wants to see this nation become what once was: God fearing, God loving, patriotic, family oriented, country lovers, and fair.

How about the poor souls that are in prison now for attending a rally and peacefully protesting. If it is against the establishment, you go to prison. If criminals protest, burn structures, kill people, burn police cars and so on and so forth, they are called peaceful protestors, and they will not set a foot in a jail. The political corruption is unbelievable. Judges, district attorneys, prosecutors, they are all pushing the same anti-Christ agenda. Well, Canada is much worse. I guess they are doing good pushing the agenda there, lol.

Therefore, brothers and sisters, we need to proclaim the gospel of our Lord and Savior Jesus Christ boldly and fearlessly, openly and honestly and truthfully. We need to save as many people as possible from the grasp of the enemy. We have the responsibility to bring as many new brothers and sisters as possible to Christ.

We as Christians know our fate, but I would not mind losing my life for my Lord and Savior Jesus Christ. He said those who lose their life for His sake will find it. Matthew 10:39 says:

"He who finds his life will lose it, and he who loses his life for My sake will find it."

On another occasion, this is what Jesus told His apostles regarding proclaiming the kingdom of God and the gospel of Jesus Christ:

"Then He said to them, 'Thus it is written, and thus it was necessary for the Christ to suffer and to rise from the dead the third day, and that repentance and remission of sins should be preached in His name to all nations, beginning at Jerusalem.'"
Luke 24:46-47

Therefore, brothers and sisters, let's proclaim the gospel of our Lord Jesus Christ boldly and courageously. God bless you. May the peace of our Lord Jesus Christ be with you. Amen.

CHAPTER EIGHT

THE RAPTURE OF THE CHURCH

The rapture of the church has been a controversial subject between churches for ages. Some denominations believe that all of us will go through the tribulation, and some don't. The rapture is briefly mentioned in the Bible, in 1 Thessalonians 4:16-17. The word rapture is believed to derived from the Greek word "Harpazo" which means "caught up" or "caught away." Let's see what Paul mentions in his first epistle to the people in Thessalonica and also to the people of Corinth.

> *"For the Lord Himself will descend from heaven with a shout, with the voice of an archangel, and with the trumpet of God. And the dead in Christ will rise first. Then we who are alive and remain shall be caught up together with them in the clouds to meet the Lord in the air. And thus we shall always be with the Lord."*
> **1 Thessalonians 4:16-17**

"Behold, I tell you a mystery: we shall not all sleep, but we shall all be changed- in a moment, in the twinkling of an eye, at the last trumpet. For the trumpet will sound, and the dead will be raised incorruptible, and we shall be changed. For this corruptible must put on incorruption, and this mortal must put on immortality."
1 Corinthians 15:51-53

Other examples of rapture are found in the Bible, such as the stories of Enoch and Elijah. In the book of Genesis and in the book of Hebrews we can find a brief recap of what happened to Enoch. We can find what happened to Elijah in the book of 2 Kings. Let's review.

"Enoch lived sixty-five years, and begot Methuselah. After he begot Methuselah, Enoch walked with God three hundred years, and had sons and daughters. So all the days of Enoch were three hundred and sixty-five years. And Enoch walked with God; and he was not, for God took him."
Genesis 5:21-24

"By faith Enoch was taken away so that he did not see death, and was not found, because God had taken him, for before he was taken he had this testimony, that he pleased God."
Hebrews 11:5

"And it came to pass, when the LORD was about to take up Elijah into heaven by a whirlwind, that Elijah went with Elisha from Gilgal."

2 Kings 2:1)

"Then it happened, as they continued on and talked, that suddenly a chariot of fire appeared with horses of fire, and separated the two of them; and Elijah went up by a whirlwind into heaven."

2 Kings 2:11

With all the evidence we have seen above, we can say that God can do anything He wants. If He wants to take us all at once in a whirlwind, or in the twinkling of an eye, He most definitely can. Based on these facts, it is difficult to mistrust the apostle Paul on what he tells us in 1 Thessalonians 4, regarding the way believers that are still alive at that time will be caught up to meet Jesus in the air. I personally believe in the rapture, based on the information we find in the scriptures. We also find that we are very close to the time for this event to take place; at any moment, we could be raptured.

Signs Before the Rapture

Are we going to see any signs before the rapture takes place? Yes, we will. In the book of Mathews, Chapter 24, we see the best explanation Jesus gave His apostles regarding the signs of the end.

> *"Now as He sat on the mount of olives, the disciples came to Him privately, saying, 'Tell us, when will these things be? And what will be the sign of your coming, and of the end of the age?' And Jesus answered and said to them: 'Take heed that no one deceives you. For many will come in My name, saying, "I am the Christ," and will deceive many. And you will hear of wars and rumors of wars. See that you are not troubled; for all these things must come to pass, but the end is not yet. For nation will rise against nation, and kingdom against kingdom. And there will be famines, pestilences, and earthquakes in various places. All these are the beginning of sorrows. Then they will deliver you up to tribulation and kill you, and you will be hated by all nations for My name's sake. And then many will be offended, will betray one another, and will hate one another. Then many false prophets will rise up and deceive many. And because lawlessness will abound, the love of many will grow cold. But he who endures to the end shall be saved. And this gospel of the kingdom will be preached in all the world as a witness to all the nations, and then the end will come.'"*

Matthew 24:3-14

What's going to happen after the rapture of the church? Will the gospel of Jesus Christ still be preached? Well, to answer the first question, what's going to happen after the rapture is written in the book of Revelation. It is called the tribulation, a seven-year period separated in two parts, one of good things that are deceptive and one of bad stuff. We will be discussing this in the next chapter. The answer to the second question can be found in the book of Revelation chapter 11.

The Two Witnesses

"Then I was given a reed like a measuring rod. And the angel stood, saying, 'Rise and measure the temple of God, the altar, and those who worship there. But leave out the court which is outside the temple, and do not measure it, for it has been given to the gentiles. And they will tread the holy city underfoot for forty-two months. And I will give power to my two witnesses, and they will prophesy one thousand two hundred and sixty days, clothed in sackcloth.'"

Revelation 11:1-3

The Proclamation of the Three Angels

"Then I saw another angel flying in the midst of heaven, having the everlasting gospel to preach to those who dwell on the earth- to every nation, tribe, tongue, and people- saying with a loud voice, 'Fear God and give glory to Him, for the hour of His judgement has come; and worship Him who made heaven and earth, the sea and the springs of water.'"

Revelation 14:6-7

As we can see, the gospel will still be preached after the church has departed. The people left behind will have the opportunity to be saved, but if I were you, I wouldn't wait until then to accept the Lord Jesus Christ as your Lord and Savior; attend a church, get baptized, and be raptured with the church of Christ.

There is a sense of urgency in the Christian world to save more lives for the glory of God, so they can go to heaven. Look at the signs; they are all over the place: on television, radio, you name it. We, the Christian community are being ostracized for proclaiming the name of our Lord Jesus Christ, for being patriotic, heck, even for speaking the truth or the obvious. It would not surprise me if we were not allowed to celebrate the 4th of July. Society has a reprobate mind.

I personally want the rapture to happen soon, the sooner the better, but on the other hand, I want it to happen later, so we can save more lost souls. That is one of the reasons God wanted me to write this book, using me as an instrument for His glory. Praise the Lord. We all have a calling in our lives; God has given each of us a talent to be use for His glory, not ours. Let's use what God has given us. Some of us know it, some don't, and some ignore it. In time, God will get your attention so you can get to it and fulfill what He wants you to do. I would not wait until that time.

This has to be one of the most exciting and anticipated events for the church of Christ. We as Christians need to rejoice for the rapture of our wonderful church of the living God. You have to know that if you were raptured, you made it to heaven. According to the scriptures, we are all going to have different crowns that will indicate our rank. I would not mind having the lowest of the ranks as long as I'm in heaven in the presence of the Lord. In addition, we will get to see and meet the prophets and all the wonderful men that wrote the books of our great Bible.

We all need to be vigilant and do the best job we can to steer people to Jesus Christ. The end is definitely near, and if you, brothers and sisters, know your loved ones are not in Christ, they need you, and they need you now. It would be very unfortunate if they miss the rapture because we did not preach to them the gospel of Jesus Christ and have them accept Him as Lord and Savior.

The signs are everywhere, brothers and sisters. Let's be ready for that glorious moment we Christians have been waiting for, the rapture of the bride of Christ, the church. God bless you.

CHAPTER NINE

THE GREAT TRIBULATION

The tribulation is the event that will take place after the rapture of the church. It is described as a seven-year period where half will be a period of what appear to be good things, and treaties with Israel which will be broken three and a half years later. The other half will be of oppression, persecution, destruction, and execution of those who don't take the mark of the beast on the right hand or the forehead. The tribulation is also associated with the day of the Lord. Let the scriptures tell us what's going to take place during that period of time, the seven years. Jesus mentioned the tribulation in the New Testament to the apostles, written in the book of Mathew chapter 24, Mark chapter 13, Luke chapters 17 and 21. It is also found in 1 Thessalonians chapter 5 and Revelation chapter 6. In addition, the tribulation is mentioned in the Old Testament by the prophets Ezekiel and Daniel. There are other references regarding the tribulation in the scriptures in both Old and New Testaments. I suggest seeking advice from a pastor, as these verses are more advance and complex. This book is intended for nonbelievers seeking God or who are caught in the in between, and for those who have just accepted Jesus Christ as their Lord and Savior. We will take a look at both the Old Testament and the New Testament. First, let us review the New Testament.

New Testament

"Therefore when you see the 'abomination of desolation,' spoken of by Daniel the prophet, standing in the holy place (whoever reads, let him understand), Then let those who are in Judea flee to the mountains. Let him who is on the housetop not go down to take anything out of his house. And let him who is in the field not go back to get his clothes. But woe to those who are pregnant and to those who are nursing babies in those days! And pray that your flight may not be in winter or on the sabbath. For then there will be great tribulation, such as has not been since the beginning of the world until this time, no, nor ever shall be. And unless those days were shortened, no flesh would be saved; but for the elect's sake those days will be shortened. Then if anyone says to you, 'Look, here is the Christ' or 'There!' do not believe it. For false Christs and false prophets will rise and show great signs and wonders to deceive, if possible, even the elect. See, I have told you

beforehand. Therefore if they say to you, 'Look, He is in the desert!' do not go out; or 'Look, He is in the inner rooms!' do not believe it. For as the lightning comes from the east and flashes to the west, so also will the coming of the Son of Man be."

Matthew 24:15-27

The description of the tribulation inMark's gospel is almost identical to the description of Mathew in his book. We will skip Mark and read the accounts of the tribulation in the book of Luke.

"Now when He was asked by the Pharisees when the kingdom of God would come, He answered them and said, "The kingdom of God does not come with observation; nor will they say, "See here!" or "See there!" For indeed, the kingdom of God is within you.' Then He said to the disciples, 'The days will come when you will desire to see one of the days of the Son of Man, and you will not see it. And they will say to you, "Look here!" or "Look there!" Do not go after them or follow them. For as the lightning that flashes out of one part under heaven shines to the other part under heaven, so also the Son of Man will be in His day. But first He must suffer many things and be rejected by this generation. And as it was in the days of Noah, so it will be also in the days of the Son of Man: They ate, they

drank, they married wives, they were given in marriage, until the day that Noah entered the ark, and the flood came and destroyed them all. Likewise as it was also in the days of Lot: They ate, they drank, they bought, they sold, they planted, they built; but on the day that lot went out of Sodom it rained fire and brimstone from heaven and destroyed them all. Even so will it be in the day when the Son of Man is revealed. In that day, he who is in the housetop, and his goods are in the house, let him not come down to take them away. And likewise the one who is in the field, let him not turn back. Remember Lot's wife. Whoever seeks to save his life will lose it, and whoever loses his life will preserve it. I tell you, in that night there will be two men in one bed: the one will be taken and the other will be left. Two women will be grinding together: the one will be taken and the other left. Two men will be in the field: the one will be taken and the other left."

Luke 17:20-36

"So they asked Him, saying, 'Teacher, but when will this thing be? And what sign will there be when these things are about to take place?' And He said: 'Take heed that you not be deceived. For many will come in My name, saying, "I am He," and, '"he time has drawn near." Therefore do not go

after them. But when you hear of wars and commotions, do not be terrified; for these things must come to pass first, but the end will not come immediately.' 10 Then He said to them, 'Nation will rise against nation, and kingdom against kingdom. And there will be great earthquakes in various places, and famines and pestilences; and there will be fearful sights and great signs from heaven. But before all these things, they will lay their hands on you and persecute you, delivering you up to the synagogues and prisons. You will be brought before kings and rulers for My name's sake. But it will turn out for you as an occasion for testimony. Therefore settle in your hearts not to mediate beforehand on what you will answer; for I will give you a mouth and wisdom which all your adversaries will not be able to contradict or resist. You will be betrayed even by parents and brothers, relatives and friends; and they will put some of you to death. And you will be hated by all for My name's sake. But not a hair of your head shall be lost. By your patience possess your souls."

Luke 21:7-19)

"For you yourselves know perfectly that the day of the Lord so comes as a thief in the night."

1 Thessalonians 5:2

Toward the end of the tribulation, the elites, the kings of the earth, the rich, and everyone who rejected the Lamb of God will try to hide from the wrath of the Lamb in the bunkers they have constructed underground, and will ask the mountains and the earth to kill them, but God Almighty will not let it happen.

> *"And the kings of the earth, the great men, the rich men, the commanders, the mighty men, every slave and every free man, hid themselves in the caves and in the rocks of the mountains, and said to the mountains and rocks, 'Fall on us and hide us from the face of Him who sits on the throne and from the wrath of the Lamb! For the great day of His wrath has come, and who is able to stand?'"*
>
> **Revelation 6:15-17**

Old Testament

> *"Alas for the day!*
> *For the day of the Lord is at hand;*
> *It shall come as destruction*
> *from the Almighty."*
>
> **(Joel 1:15)**

> *"Blow the trumpet in Zion,*
> *And sound an alarm in*
> *My holy mountain!*

Let all the inhabitants of
the land tremble;
For the day of the Lord is coming,
For it is at hand:
A day of darkness and gloominess,
A day of clouds and thick darkness,
Like the morning clouds spread
over the mountains.
And people come, great and strong,
The like of whom has never been;
Nor will there ever be any
such after them,
Even for many successive generations.
A fire devours before them,
And behind them a flame burns;
* The land is like the Garden*
of Eden before them,
And behind them a desolate wilderness;
Surely nothing shall escape them.
Their appearance is like the
appearance of horses;
And like swift steeds, so they run.
With a noise like chariots
Over mountaintops they leap,

Like the of a flaming fire

that devours the stubble,

Like a strong people set in battle array.

Before them the people writhe in pain;

All faces are drained of color.

They run like mighty men,

They climb the wall like men of war;

Every one marches in formation,

And they do not break ranks.

They do not push one another;

Every one marches in his own column.

Though they lunge between the weapons,

They are not cut down.

They run to and fro in the city,

They run on the wall;

They climb into the houses,

They enter at the windows like a thief.

The earth quakes before them,

The heavens tremble;

The sun and the moon grow dark,

And the stars diminished their brightness.

The LORD gives voice before His army,

For His camp is very great;

For strong is the One who

executes His word.
For the day of the LORD is
great and very terrible;
Who can endure it?"

Joel 2:1-11

Now, let's see what the prophets Daniel and Jeremiah say:

> *"At that time Michael shall stand up, The great prince who stands watch over the sons of your people; And there shall be a time of trouble, such as never was since there was a nation, Even to that time. And at that time your people shall be delivered, Every one who is found written on the book."*

Daniel 12:1

> *"Alas! For that day is great, so that none is like it; And it is the time of Jacob's trouble, But he shall be saved out of it."*

Jeremiah 30:7

The Anti-Christ

Now we are going to read about the anti-Christ in the scriptures, since we know he will be controlling the world during and prior to the great tribulation. Actually, he's controlling now. Let's read so we can understand the signs of his appearance in the world stage. We will go to the first epistle of John.

> *"Little children, it is the last hour; and as you have heard that the Antichrist is coming, even now many antichrists have come, by which we know that it is the last hour. They went out from us, but they were not of us; for if they had been of us, they would have continued with us; but they went out that they be manifest, that none of them were of us. But you have an anointing from the Holy One, and you know all things. I have not written to you because you do not know the truth, but because you know it, and no lie is of the truth. Who is a liar but he who denies that Jesus is the Christ? He is antichrist who denies the Father and the Son. Whoever denies the Son does not have the Father either; he who acknowledges the Son has the Father also.*
>
> **1 John 2:18-23**

> *"Then he shall confirm a covenant with many for one week; But in the middle of the week He shall bring an end to sacrifice and offering. And on the wing of abominations shall be one who makes desolate, Even until the consummation, which is determined, Is poured out on the desolate."*
>
> **Daniel 9:27**

Well, brothers and sisters, this concludes this chapter of the great tribulation. God bless you!

CHAPTER TEN

THE SECOND COMING OF CHRIST

This has to be the most exciting chapter to talk about. We will be reviewing the scriptures to find out what they say regarding the greatest event in history, which is about to happen, very shortly, I hope. That is: the second coming of our Lord Jesus Christ, which is so exciting for us, the Christian community, the true believers. The most expected part of the second coming of our Lord, is the first stop Jesus makes before setting foot on the earth, which is to pick up His Bride, the church, us, in the event called the rapture. Let's see what the scriptures say about the second coming of our Lord and Savior Jesus Christ. We will read from both Testaments.

The New Testament

"Immediately after the tribulation of those days the sun will darkened, and the moon will not give its light; the stars will fall from

heaven, and the powers of the heavens will be shaken. Then the sign of the Son of Man will appear in heaven, and then all tribes of the earth will mourn, and they will see the Son of Man coming on the clouds of heaven with power and great glory. And He will send His angels with a great sound of a trumpet, and they will gather together His elect from the four winds, from one end of heaven to the other."

Matthew 24:29-31

John tells us in his book what Jesus said to the apostles regarding His second coming, in John 14:1-4:

" 'Let not your heart be troubled; you believe in God, believe also in Me. In My Father's house are many mansions; if it were not so, I would have told you. I go to prepare a place for you. And if I go and prepare a place for you, I will come again and receive you Myself; that where I am, there you may be also. And where I go you know, and the way you know.' "

John 14:1-4

" 'But of that day and hour no one knows, not even the angels in heaven, nor the Son, but only the Father. Take heed, watch and pray; for you do not know when the time is. It is like a man going to a far country, who left

his house and gave authority to his servants, and to each his work, and commanded the doorkeeper to watch. Watch therefore, for you do not know when the master of the house is coming – lest, coming suddenly, he finds you sleeping. And what I say to you, I say to all: Watch!'"

Mark 13:32-37

"'And there will be signs in the sun, in the moon, and in the stars; and on the earth distress of nations, with perplexity, the sea and the waves roaring; men's hearts failing from fear and the expectation of those things which are coming on the earth, for the powers of the heavens will be shaken. Then they will see the Son of Man coming in a cloud with power and great glory. Now when these things begin to happen, look up and lift up your heads, because your redemption draws near.' Then He spoke to them a parable: 'Look at the fig tree, and all the trees. When they are already budding, you see and know for yourselves that summer is now near. So you also, when you see these things happening, know that the kingdom of God is near. Assuredly, I say to you, this generation will by no means pass away till all things take place. Heaven and earth will pass away, but My words will by no means pass away. But take heed to yourselves, lest your hearts be

weighed down with carousing, drunkenness, and cares of this life, and that Day come on you unexpectedly. For it will come as a snare on all those who dwell on the face of the whole earth. Watch therefore, and pray always that you may be counted worthy to escape all these things that will come to pass, and to stand before the Son of Man.'"

Luke 21:25-36

"Now when He had spoken these things, while they watch, He was taken up, and a cloud received Him out of their sight. And while they looked steadfastly toward heaven as He went up, behold, two men stood by them in white apparel, who also said, 'Men of Galilee, why do you stand gazing up into heaven? This same Jesus, who was taken up from you into heaven, will so come in like manner as you saw Him go into heaven.'"

Acts 1:9-11

"For the Lord Himself will descend from heaven with a shout, with the voice of an archangel, and with the trumpet of God. And the dead in Christ will rise first. Then we who are alive and remain shall be caught up together with them in the clouds to meet the Lord in the air. And thus we shall always be with the Lord. Therefore comfort one another with these words."

1 Thessalonians 4:16-18

"But, beloved, do not forget this one thing, that with the Lord one day is as a thousand years, and a thousand years as one day. The Lord is not slack concerning His promise, as some count slackness, but is longsuffering toward us, not willing that any should perish but that all should come to repentance."

2 Peter 3:8-9

"...and to give you who are troubled rest with us when the Lord Jesus is revealed from heaven with His mighty angels, in flaming fire taking vengeance on those who do not know God, and on those who do not obey the gospel of our Lord Jesus Christ. These shall be punished with everlasting destruction from the presence of the Lord and from the glory of His power, when He comes, in that day, to be glorified in His saints and to be admired among all those who believe, because our testimony among you was believed."

2 Thessalonians 1:7-10

"Behold, He is coming with clouds, and every eye will see Him, even they who pierced Him. And all the tribes of the earth will mourn because of Him. Even so. Amen. 'I am the Alpha and the Omega, the Beginning and the End,' says the Lord, 'Who is and who was is to come, the Almighty.'"

Revelation 1:7-8

These references are from the New Testament. As we can see, they are powerful testimonies of the second coming of our wonderful Lord Jesus Christ. I don't need to remind you that the day is getting close, as we have confirmed in the scriptures. Most of what we need to know for that time that is to come is there. Therefore, immerse yourselves in the scriptures.

Another subject worth mentioning is the battle of Armageddon.

> *"Then the sixth angel sounded: And I heard a voice from the four horns of the golden altar which is before God, saying to the sixth angel who had the trumpet, 'Release the four angels who are bound at the great river Euphrates.' So the four angels, who had been prepared for the hour and the day and the month and year, were released to kill a third of mankind. Now the number of the army of the horsemen was two hundred million; I heard the number of them."*
> **Revelation 9:13-16**

> *"Then the sixth angel poured out his bowl on the great river Euphrates, and its water was dried up, so that the way of the kings of the east might be prepared. And I saw three unclean spirits like frogs coming out the mouth of the dragon, out of the mouth of the beast, and out of the mouth of the false prophet. or they are*

spirits of demons, performing signs, which go out of the kings of the earth and of the whole world, to gather them to the battle of the great day of God Almighty. 'Behold, I am coming as a thief. Blessed is he who watches, and keep his garments, lest he walk naked and they see his shame.' And they gather them together to the place called in Hebrew, Armageddon."
Revelation 16:12-16

The Old Testament

Now let's read what the Old Testament says about the second coming of our Messiah. Most of the mentions of the second coming of Jesus in the Old Testament have to do with returning Israel to their land (the rest of it), after Christ has come back to earth and has judged the nations.

" 'But you, Bethlehem Ephrathah, though you are little among the thousands of Judah, yet out of you shall come forth to Me the One to be ruler of Israel, Whose goings forth are from of old, From everlasting.' "
Micah 5:2

"...and you return to the LORD your God and obey His voice, according to all that I command you today, you and your children, with all your heart and with all your soul, that the LORD your God will bring you back from captivity, and have compassion on you, and

gather you again from all the nations where the LORD your God has scattered you."

Deuteronomy 30:2-3

"'For behold, the days are coming,' says the LORD, 'that I will bring back from captivity My people Israel and Judah,' says the LORD. 'And I will cause them to return to the land that I gave to their fathers, and they shall possess it.'"

Jeremiah 30:3

"I will bring the captives of my people Israel; They shall build the waste cities and inhabit them; They shall plant vineyards and drink wine from them; They shall also make gardens and eat fruit from them. I will plant them in their land, And no longer they shall be pulled up from the land I have given them,' says the LORD your God."

Amos 9:14-15

"Now therefore, be wise, O kings; be instructed, you judges of the earth.

Serve the LORD with fear, And rejoice with trembling.

Kiss the Son, lest He be angry, and you perish in the way, When His wrath is kindled but a little. Bless are those who put the trust in Him."

Psalm 2:10-12

"Lift up your heads, O you gates! And be lifted up, you everlasting doors! And the king of glory shall come in.

Who is the king of glory? The LORD strong and mighty, the LORD mighty in battle.

Lift up your heads, O you gates! Lift up, you everlasting doors! And the king of glory shall come in.

Who is the king of glory? The LORD of hosts, He is the king of glory."

Psalm 24:7-10

"Give your king your judgement, O God, And your righteousness to the king's Son.

He will judge Your people with righteousness, And your poor with justice.

The mountains will bring peace to the people, And the little hills, by righteousness.

He will bring justice to the poor of the people, He will save the children of the needy, And will break in pieces the oppressor.

They shall fear You As long as the sun and the moon endure, Throughout all generations.

He shall come down like rain upon the grass before mowing, Like showers that waters the earth.

In His days the righteous shall flourish, And abundance of peace, Until the moon is no more.

He shall have dominion also from sea to sea, And from River to the ends of the earth.

Those who dwell in the wilderness will bow before Him, And His enemies will leak the dust.

10 The kings of Tarshish and of the isles Will bring presents; The kings of Sheba and Seba will offer gifts.

Yes, all kings shall fall down before Him; All nations shall serve Him."

Psalm 72:1-11

"Say among the nations, 'The LORD reigns; The world is also firmly established, it shall not be moved; He shall judge the peoples righteously.'

Let the heavens rejoice, and let the earth be glad; Let the sea roar, and all its fullness;

Let the field be joyful, and all that is in it. Then all the trees of the woods will rejoice before the LORD.For He is coming, for He is coming to judge the earth. He shall judge the world with righteousness, And the people with His truth."

Psalm 96:10-13

"The LORD said to my Lord, 'Sit at my right hand, Till I make your enemies Your

footstool.'

The LORD shall send the rod of Your strength out of Zion. Rule in the midst of Your enemies!

Your people shall be volunteers In the day of Your power; In the beauties of holiness, from the womb of the morning, You have the dew of Your youth.

The LORD has sworn And will not relent, 'You are a priest forever According to the order of Melchizedek.'

The Lord is at Your right hand; He shall execute kings in the day of His wrath.

He shall judge among the nations, He shall fill the places with dead bodies, he shall execute the heads of many countries.

He shall drink of the brook by the wayside; Therefore He shall lift up the head."
Psalm 110:1-7

Brothers and sisters, stay vigilant and in prayer. This is the conclusion of my efforts to bring you a little guidance. Thank You, Holy Spirit, for guiding me through this great experience, for the glory of God Almighty.

In a lost world, we need all the help we can get. Read the scriptures diligently.

May God bless all of you.

Printed in the USA
CPSIA information can be obtained
at www.ICGtesting.com
CBHW071823300724
12432CB00025B/660